MICHAEL

THE
WO

CUBS

COLLINS COLOUR CUBS

ELTON Woofit was sure he wanted to be a pop star until he met Baskerville Woofit. Then he decided he would rather be a newspaper reporter.

Baskerville was an elderly man with a red nose and a large stomach. He always wore a shabby raincoat and a trilby hat with the brim turned down.

He dressed like this because when he was a youngster, newspaper reporters – at least the ones he saw on the American movies – always dressed like this.

Times had changed, but not Baskerville. He lived in the past when he was an ace reporter on a big London newspaper.

He loved telling stories about his adventures, and Elton loved listening to them. Elton liked the war stories best of all.

"Tell us about what happened in the war, Uncle Baskerville," said Elton one day as they sat in the Woofits' living-room.

John Willy Woofit, Elton's father, groaned because he had heard it all so many times before.

Angela Woofit, Elton's sister (who was taking elocution lessons because she wanted to be a newsreader on the television) sighed and left the room. She thought Uncle Baskerville was boring and far too ugly to read the News on television.

"It was very rough," said Uncle Baskerville, pushing his hat on to the back of his head. "I landed with the commandos – and they were a tough bunch of lads, I can tell you. Bullets were flying all around the landing-craft. We had to wade ashore for the last hundred yards. There we were – neck-deep in water – sitting targets for the enemy."

"Didn't the soldiers get their guns wet?" asked Elton.

"No. Carried them above their heads as they waded ashore," said Baskerville.

"Were *you* carrying a gun above *your* head?" asked Elton.

Baskerville Woofit looked a bit uncomfortable.

"Well, actually – no. I carried my typewriter above my head," he said.

Elton thought his father was going to die laughing. John Willy slapped his thighs and laughed until the tears streamed down his cheeks.

"Stop it, John Willy,or you'll have one of your turns," said Mrs Woofit, who was knitting a scarf for Elton.

"What's so funny?" demanded Baskerville huffily.

"You attacking the enemy with a typewriter!" said John Willy between laughs.

"Some people have a peculiar sense of humour," said Baskerville with dignity.

Elton didn't think it was funny either. He was picturing himself as a war correspondent, being decorated for bravery under fire.

"I think I'd like to be a reporter," he said.

Next day, he went into his parents' wardrobe and tried on his father's old mac. It was much too big for him but that didn't bother Elton. He was determined to look the part.

He looked for a trilby hat, but could only find a flat cap which he tried on, but decided it didn't look right.

He even tried the peaked cap his father wore when he played with the brass band.

That made him look like a traffic warden.

He went downstairs in the raincoat.
"Our Elton, you look proper wet!" said Angela who was practising her elocution.

Elton ignored her and went out of the house.

He caught a bus to the High Street. The other passengers gave him strange looks as he got on wearing his outsize raincoat.

Elton paid no attention.

When he left the bus he went straight to the office where his Uncle Baskerville worked. He went into the newsroom where the reporters were working at their desks.

They were all typing like mad and the air was full of the chatter of their machines.

He spotted his uncle.

Baskerville Woofit was sitting staring at his typewriter, his trilby pushed to the back of his head.

"Where did you get the raincoat?" he asked Elton.

"I borrowed it from Dad," said Elton.

"Is it raining, then?" asked Baskerville.

"No. It's my uniform," said Elton.

"Uniform?" exclaimed Baskerville.

"Yes, my reporter's uniform. I want to be a newspaperman like you."

His uncle was flattered. He stuck his thumbs in his braces and asked:

"Then how can I help you?"

"By lending me your hat," said Elton.

"There's more to being a reporter than wearing a raincoat and a hat," frowned Baskerville.

"I know, but I've got to start somewhere," said Elton.

Uncle Baskerville opened the drawer of his desk and pulled out a brand new hat.

"I was going to throw my old one away and wear this one," he said, "but you can have it for a day or so."

Elton thanked him and put the hat on his head. It was much too big, and but for his ears holding it up, would have covered his face.

"What do I do now?" asked Elton.

"Same as all good reporters," said Uncle Baskerville with a smile. "Go and find me a story. And, by gum, I need one!" he added.

When Elton reached home his mother looked up from her knitting and said: "Oh dear, Elton, what have you done to yourself?"

Elton explained about his career as a reporter.

"What will you do?" she asked.

"I'll go to the police station and ask if they've got a story for me," he said. "I'll go on my bike."

"Your new hat will fall off," giggled Angela.

Elton looked worried.

But his mother was used to coping with problems. She sewed a piece of elastic to either side of the trilby.

"It won't come off now," she said, putting the hat on Elton's head and fixing the elastic under his chin.

It was uphill all the way to the police station but there was a strong wind at Elton's back. His long coat flapped and billowed like a sail in the wind.

The police station was a modern building, all brick and glass. Elton parked his cycle and went inside.

There was a large desk, and behind the desk an even larger policeman with friendly blue eyes and the largest moustache Elton had ever seen.

"Now then, young man," he boomed, "name please."

"Elton Woofit," said Elton.

"Well, mine is Sergeant Fox," said the policeman, "not to be confused with box, cox, or sox."

He started to shake with laughter. He was enjoying his favourite joke. Then he straightened up and said to Elton:

"What can I do for you?"

"I want a story," said Elton.

The sergeant looked surprised.

Elton told the sergeant all about his ambition to be a newspaper reporter. When he had finished, the sergeant stroked his whiskers thoughtfully.

"Well," he said, "I think you're probably a bit young to be a reporter but I've no doubt you will be, one day."

The sergeant could see Elton was disappointed.

"However," he said, "I know you have an uncle who is a reporter so you can tell him to ring me up and I'll give him a red-hot story. I'll tell him it's all thanks to you. OK?"

Elton was thrilled. He ran out of the police station, nearly tripping over his long raincoat, and jumped on his bike.

He set off down the hill at a furious rate.

He was pedalling into a strong wind and all of a sudden his hat started to rise up from his head. Because of the chin-strap, it didn't fly off, but the elastic stretched and stretched until the hat soared above Elton like a parachute.

Suddenly the elastic snapped and the hat flew high in the air. It circled and spun in the wind, and then fell in the roadway.

Elton stopped and was about to go back for his Uncle Baskerville's new hat when he saw a large red van coming down the hill.

There was nothing he could do but watch in horror as the van ran over the hat and then roared away down the hill.

When Elton picked up the hat it was as flat as a pancake and covered in mud.

What would he tell Uncle Baskerville?

He made his way back to the office.
He found his uncle still staring at his typewriter. He looked very gloomy.
"Well, how did our ace reporter do?" he asked.

"All right," said Elton, wondering how he would tell Uncle Baskerville about his hat. "What sort of a day did *you* have, Uncle?"

"Terrible!" said Uncle Baskerville. "Nothing happening. I haven't got a story."

"I've got one for you," said Elton.
Baskerville brightened and took his feet off the desk.
Elton told his uncle about his talk with Sergeant Fox.
"Great!" said Baskerville. "I'll ring him at once – then I'll buy you a lemonade."

Elton waited while Baskerville made the call. Then he said:

"That was the good news. I've got some bad news, too."

He told his uncle about the hat, and about the elastic, and about the big red van.

Uncle Baskerville could just picture it. He laughed. He laughed a lot.

"Don't worry, Elton," he said. "I didn't like that hat anyway. You got the best story of the week. It'll make the front page."

When Elton got home, his father was sitting in a corner, polishing his trombone.

Angela was watching the News on television and wondering if she would be better than the lady newsreader.

Mrs Woofit was still knitting the scarf for Elton. It was getting very long.

"You look proper daft in my raincoat," said John Willy Woofit.

"No he doesn't. He looks lovely!" said Mrs Woofit.

"Our Elton's a real mess," said Angela, her eyes never leaving the television.

Elton went upstairs and put his father's coat back in the wardrobe.

He was feeling exhausted after his day's adventures.

He went to his bedroom and picked up his guitar.

He sat there for a long time, just thinking.

Next morning, Uncle Baskerville's story was splashed all over the front page of the *Daily Woofit*.

Elton sighed. Being a reporter was really too much of a strain.

He would go back to being a pop star.

As seen on ITV
With acknowledgment to
TRIDENT TELEVISION LIMITED
ISBN 0 00 123529 X

Printed in Great Britain.